ALSO BY RAVI SHANKAR

Deepening Groove
Winner of the National Poetry Review Prize
(TNPR, 2011)

Seamless Matter
(Ohm Editions, Rain Taxi Books, 2010)

Voluptuous Bristle
(Finishing Line, 2010)

Radha Says
posthumous collection by Reetika Vazirani
(Drunken Boat Media, 2010)

*Language for a New Century: Contemporary Poetry
from Asia, the Middle East & Beyond*
(W.W. Norton & Co., 2008)

Wanton Textiles
(No Tell Books, 2006)

Instrumentality
Finalist for the Connecticut Book Awards
(Cherry Grove, 2004)

Series Editor: Andrea Selch

Design: Lesley Landis Designs

Cover Image: "Smoke Painting # 38" ©2013
    courtesy of Rosemarie Fiore Studio

Author Photograph: Oil painting by Michael J. Peery ©2014
    photographed by Larry St. Pierre

The mission of Carolina Wren Press is to seek out, nurture and promote literary work by new and underrepresented writers, including women and people of color.

Carolina Wren Press is a 501(c)3 nonprofit organization supported in part by grants and generous individual donors. This publication was made possible by a grant from the North Carolina Arts Council as well as ongoing support made possible through gifts to the Durham Arts Council's United Arts Fund.

Library of Congress Cataloging-in-Publication Data

Shankar, Ravi, 1975-
[Poems. Selections]
What else could it be : ekphrastics & collaborations / by Ravi Shankar.
pages ; cm. -- (Poetry series ; #17)
ISBN 978-0-932112-92-7
I. Title.

PS3619.H3547A6 2015
811'.6--dc23

2015005987

What Else Could It Be:
Ekphrastics and Collaborations

Ravi Shankar

Poetry Series #17

CAROLINA WREN PRESS
Durham, North Carolina

ACKNOWLEDGMENTS

The author would like to thank the MacDowell Colony, Djerassi Resident Artists Program, the Blue Mountain Center, the Jentel Foundation, the Jackson Hole Writers Conference, the Stonecoast Writers' Conference, the Wesleyan Writers Conference, Central Connecticut State University, and City University of Hong Kong for their support toward the completion of this manuscript. Abundant gratitude for my friends and family who have furnished my life with the substance and buoyancy it needs to allow these poems to arrive, and to my numerous collaborators who helped channel something improvisational that would not exist without our distinctive call and response. This applies also to those artists, living and dead, whose work engendered the ekphrastic poems. The polyphonic nexus of creative energy we partake in links us back through the past to each other. A special thank you to Julie Batten for her love and inspiration, to Sharon Dolin for providing suggestions for revision, to Michael J. Peery for his meticulous rendering of my portrait over many months, to Robert Dowling, Rand Richards Cooper, Daniel Donaghy, Tom Hazuka, Lisa Russ Spaar, Katherine Sugg, and Andy Thibault for providing friendship when I most needed it, to Sybil Baker, Tina Chang, Evan Fallenberg, Luis Francia, James Scudamore, Xu Xi, and the rest of the faculty at City University of Hong Kong for their dedicated support, to Jim Finnegan and the Brickwalk Writing Group for their perceptive comments on drafts of these poems, to Diane Creede, Rajni Shankar-Brown, Rahini Shankar, Rajee Shankar and K.H. Shankar for their unwavering loyalty, and to my daughters Samara and Talia for helping give my life meaning and delight. I couldn't have written this without all of you!

The author also wishes to thank Andrea Selch and Robin Miura, codirectors of Carolina Wren Press, as well as the editors, curators, and publishers of the following publications and art projects in which poems from this collection have appeared or are forthcoming as follows:

Almost Island: "Course of Empire" and "The Two Fridas"

Ambit: "Blue Circus"

The Asia Literary Review: "All Tomorrow's Ancestors," "The Shanty of Subliminal Governance," "Singapore Spring," "The River of Palms," and "Tempo Rubato Luminoso Con Moto, or: Notes from the Field Guide of Postlapsarian Instruction"

The Awl: "Love and Decay"

The AWP *Writer's Chronicle*: "Last Turn on the Left"

Bloodaxe Book of Contemporary Indian Poets: "A Square of Blue Infinity"

Bryant Literary Review: "The Third of May"

Carte Blanche: "The Theory of Radioactivity"

Cha: "The Castle Looms Blue"

Cimarron Review: "Movements"

Columbia: "Sea Watchers"

Connotations Press: "Heirlooms"

Ekphrasis: "Untitled (PH-58)"

Fulcrum: "A Square of Blue Infinity"

Green Mountains Review: "Glass-Bottomed Boat" and "Desert Math"

Hinchas de Poesia: "Architect Attacked by a Goshawk, or the Unsilent Night" and "As Slow as Possible"

London Calling: An Anthology of Poems: "Sounds like Traxx"

Maine Magazine: "Emergency Egress and Exits"

Mead—the Magazine of Literature and Libations: "Route 66 Motels"

New Haven Review: "Ephemerality = Permanence"

New Pony: A Horse Less Anthology: "Something about Grandfathers," also published in *Smith Blue* by Camille Dungy (Southern Illinois University Press, 2011)

No Tell Motel: "Wanton Textiles," also published as part of a collaborative chapbook with Reb Livingston (No Tell Books, 2006)

Omniverse: "Funk & Wag: Revivals to Schopenhauer," commissioned by Mel Chin and reprinted in *The Funk and Wag from A to Z (Menil Collection)*, *Yale University Press*

Prairie Schooner: "Maine Islands"

Qarrtsiluni: "Sound Is a Chance Operation" (published as "Scraping through the Loop")

Redactions: "The Living Trust Mill"

Scythe: "Untitled (Rothko)"

Sinatra:…but buddy, I'm a kind of poem: "The Day the Voice Died"

The Southampton Review: "I could no longer play I could no longer play by instinct"

Spork: "Sounds Like Traxx"

Taos Journal of Poetry and Art: "Frame and Snare Drum" and "Two Water Towers Red"

Theodate: "The Tub"

Tuesday: An Art Project: "Rodeo Cowboy"

Urhalpool: "New York City"

TABLE OF CONTENTS

3.

to
K.H. & Rajee Shankar
for allowing me
in spite of unconformity
to love art

1.

If you understood everything I said, you'd be me.

—MILES DAVIS

Blue Circus (1950)

Mine alone is the land
that exists in my soul
I enter it without a passport
like I do my own home
—Marc Chagall

Polymorphous saturation
    oh blue
  space, river without banks
    speculum mundi
  there's a cock in the corner
     banging a drum
  fish with a sly eye
head a bed for supple coupling
    horse in green, coquette
     lovingly decapitated
  by cerulean shadow
    mane preened
       cooping up a man
     delirious moon on violin
  flecked orb, yellow orchestral
      depthless dancing
    to horn, cello, accordion
  ring-wrangling Mediterranean nymph
    oh blue
     lumière liberté
   in a diagonal swath
  a trapeze-artist swims
    upside down, rouged
      peacock crowned
  belly round, breasts round
    like a prayer
   that sometimes ends
     in laughter

Something about Grandfathers

with Camille Dungy

Fit a fastener around inside and out,
twist it tight, then tighter, until intent

bulges to bursting, the way an eyeball (cartoon)
pops from the face of a strangled boy. Consider

a Christmas menagerie, complete with plastic
wise men carrying neon frankincense

and fool's gold. Gold and something
we'll call myrrh. This is how we hold on.

Because hope can satirize itself yet remain
sincere, devout. Your mother has you up before dawn

because it's Easter. Worship before eggs
and ham and all of this and that. Hold on

like this. Or some other way, say with a shoe-
box full of her father's military medals,

the slim portion of him you knew flattened in tin
and ribbon. Hold the ribbon like a subway strap

because this car is moves, shudders on rails
faster than a voice floating above a staircase

that belonged once to him who might call
you by that pet-name, might break you some brittle

in calloused hands were you to climb the stairs.
Hold on. Who's gone? The estimated average

is greater than one death per second. Wave
upon particular wave, incessant. Even ritual,

which is what we have to cope with, breaks down
like candy in a fist. Faster. Soon. Even this

thought, fear not, will be gone like dust
into piles, into bins, like air from the cheeks

into a trumpet's bell, fuzzed by a mute into movement
that charges the room electric before the old man

in overalls brings out the mop. Gone like 8-tracks
wound down to a stretched out voice slowing

to crawl as a tape deck shreds tape.
After the car door closes to leave an echo

hanging in the canyon where it was shouted,
the red fields grow burred, then broken in snow.

All Tomorrow's Ancestors

with Alvin Pang

Burnt-out taxis rust like lozenges on a tongue of rain,
the road last travelled barely road, nearly desert now,
parched coarse as a lunar surface, erasing the footprints

of people whose ancestors once drank yak's milk tea.
Prayer flags, hunting horns, folk remedies, a child's first toy
on the broken counter, coins spilt unsmiling on the floor

to oxidize coppery green in the ensuing years with a value
far from intrinsic. If those relics store a certain ritual
magic, a way of perceiving the world foreign to the wired

generation, then to tap the trapped energies outwits time.
Time was, Grandpa says, the sea came all the way up
here, where your uncle lost his faith to silence. Its ebb

a breaking into form as of a canvas marred by paint
to create another wholeness. Stained hours, fibrous days
the span of sutures between bones of the skull

glimpsed through teeming blood cells unsensed
by microscope for millennia until an unschooled
Dutch linen-draper stretched soda-lime glass in a flame

to magnify a universe of corkscrewing cascading
microbial creatures in a single drop of pond water.
See, we all came up, the way was time, says Grandpa

wrapped in a blanket, gesticulating eyes turned inward,
here, where faith lost silence, the shoreline abrades
the ear. What do we know of time but its departures?

The fossil air stiffens into breeze, into heat, folds light
over itself in waves, impossible to trace without smearing
the instruments with agency. Particularizing whatever will be.

Rodeo Cowboy No. 1 (1978)

Subject-matter is at best a vehicle to transcend
—Fritz Scholder

Giddy up pigment! Ride them blue horse!
In a dervish
                        of dust that disquiets
                                    the limbs
hoof like a boot   spur on the flank
tail a trail   that recedes into green hills
            whole organism launched in mid-air
without crowdnoise   without leatherburn
                        depth an occluded measurement
vertiginous   rider a totemic showman
                        back turned
                                    faceless
                                            hint of a brim
day an overall yolkyellow flattened dimensionless
animal and man primal   less the primacy of paint

Maine Islands (1938)

a gathering of words of other fondled words begotten is called investigation, and this
in turn is called cerebral rapture
—Mardsen Hartley

Rough edged wilderness, all crag, surf, pines & sky,
a land before the lobstermen, logging crews, iron works,

& Acadians had bent the natural shapes into commerce,
before the radiocarbon dated Red Paint People some say

according to medieval Rabbinic fables descended from one
of the lost tribes of Israel yet who gouged out mollusks

with flaked stone, hunted swordfish & buried their own
in graves of red ocher—*when the surf licks with its tongues*—

before the Paleo-Indians followed musk ox & caribou,
wooly mammoths & giant bison across the Bering Land

Bridge into Alaska & through a corridor between glaciers
leaving behind a trail of spear tips with fluted points,

but after the last glaciation had receded to leave turbulent
brush-strokes—*these volcanic personal shapes*—a flat plane

between foreground & background with no sign of human
presence—*which we defining for ourselves as rocks accept them*

as such—the horizon bathed blue when clouds shrink
above the serrated treeline & below the chunky, brown

& slate, grainy, Cezannesque earth—its *feverish incoming*—
a primitivist landscape, part physical presence deliberately

stitch-stroked onto canvas, part transcendent intermediary
between air & infinite space—*those restless entities disturbing*

solid substances—that emerges from the view that predates
sight, making the stubble of dried paint a mood of longing,

like the secret mourning of a man for his Nazi German
officer lover killed fighting on the front & never replaced

from the center of a restless, peripatetic existence in quest
of something purer—*a curious, irrelevant, common fret*—

where landscape's lack of depth has its own depthlessness
& the sea like the past recedes & approaches, palpitates,

a place like Vinalhaven, Isle au Haut, Mantinicus, Hupper
& off into the Cisco Bay. A place starker & more isolated

than now, dangerous—*the inwash cooling at least the eye*—
yet lyric in its childlike grandeur hung to see in a frame.

The Living Trust Mill

with Jim Daniels

The discordance between thinking and thought
occurred just after the knockout punch
but before he hit the canvas.
Floodlights met deer in headlights,
mouthpiece a momentary parabola dripping spit
in camera flash and crowd roar. He had no shot
in any court of law. He was guilty, guilty,
and who couldn't count from one to ten?

Even the orphan child and the cute dog shook
their heads and walked away. Ambled out like amber waves
of green. Every payout had its outfit, even fitness
drinks debated in the boardroom were engorged on power-
point pie charts and a dream of MORE destination vacations
than any mere mortal could muster. Money in drinkable form,
dehydrated coins, capsulated dollar bills. Power, fitness,
fitness, power. *Gimme another piece of that pie. The one,*
the chewy one, the crunchy one, the juicy one.
The cartoon pie, the moon pie. The shy pie.
Gimme the last piece of the last pie. Not rarified words

like transnational and monetary policy. Just "I'm going to get me mine," like Keith Sweat
crooned. Unfortunately
the moment is not just self-reflective, contains Gambians
unlit, unctuous with sweat, unregistered by green card,
scouring pots in the basement of a French Bistro
in the meatpacking district. Like Keith Croon sweating
and swearing, scouring and glowering, some giant Somebody
pinching out their light like a nubby candle
after a long night of quiet wine, the solemn ceremony
of obliteration, limbs and teeth lulled to sleep.

The holy relic of the green card, a sliver of the one true green card wrapped in tissue, lift-
ed to a place of solitary worship, the absurdly clean hands praying for a worthy scam.
Like the man in a slick suit selling annuities to men in plaid pants: Fixed, immediate,

variable, deferred, equity-indexed. New forms for bilking. We're all grist for the living
trust mill. How much would you pay

someone not to be paid to clean ditches and bale crops
in Death Valley midday? Just sign on the dotted line,
an X is fine. Stick, stack, sloe-eyed seamstress
in a sweatshop while bee-bop skittles on no radio station in earshot. Just the drone of
needles. Hope evaporating into gray sky's hollow drone. A man rocking on a stoop closes
his eyes and remembers vision.

Imagine someone whittling his bones for kindling
or to carve an even smaller man. Imagine someone
calling this a job. Instead, while wayang puppets dance punch-drunk, imagine the seven
tones of metallophones, bamboo flutes and brass gongs that comprise the gamelan. From
the Javanese "to hammer." Shimmered sound
the frequency of a distant planet's orbit.
A communal act, job of another hue.

The sun bites into our small rotations of hope.
We shade our eyes against it. We steer our spaceships
toward dazzling music, the sweet darkness where all
is lost. Keening oboe and bassoon obbligati.
Boosters and fuel tanks dropping through atmosphere
to ocean floor, shard of ship receding into pulsating
reaches of nothingness. How the fact of its trajectory
shares an event horizon with both chauffeured
man and dark man who cleans out the discharge
cylinders of slurry pumps, then leaves in a rented van.
The chauffeured man is deep in thought.
The dark man is thinking.

Ephemerality = Permanence

with Lena Kallergi

Each reading of your palm a different road
verging from soil and forking into possibilities
in a wild and foreign ocean
no vaster than the line it makes with the sky
changing with touch
to resemble a soap bubble's rim—
how it trails, surfaces illusion,
peppers translucence with lids
of water underneath the skin
layered with centuries of silt and smelt—
sea of the past, rivers of tomorrow
branch backwards in tributaries that
cannot be named and will not stay.
I know no secret that won't sail away
so come with me, where
no knot not nautical in nature
binds us like twisting sheets to a cleat.

Sea Watchers (1952)

I find in working, always the distracting intrusion of elements not a part of my most interested vision, and the inevitable obliteration and replacement of this vision by the work itself as it proceeds.
—Edward Hopper

Not the Hamptons, even a half-century ago,
more barren in midday than a beach should be,
gull-less, garrulous only on the clothesline
where orange and yellow towels flutter dry.

Impassive as the angular stones in the sand,
husband and wife steep in the sun, silent.
It's been years since they felt any need
for small talk and now, childless, on vacation,

they've chosen a concrete shore house
to spend a week swimming, eating lobster
rolls at the shack in the center of town,
and watching the clear hyaline sea darken

in spots over the kelp-encrusted rocks.
At night, she will undress, carefully folding
her navy blue two-piece swimsuit over
the porcelain lip of the streaked claw-foot

tub that stands adjacent to the narrow bed
where he reclines, reading a *Popular Mechanics*.
She will unhook the clasp of the swim cap
under her chin to shake out her still damp

hair, to frown fractionally at the mirror
before getting into bed. In a few minutes,
he will place the magazine in the bedside
table's oak drawer, click off the lamp,

and without exchanging a word, hold her
by the ankles to better gain purchase
on the taut cotton sheets she will remake
in the morning when he jogs on the beach.

Heirlooms

with Terri Witek

Castle looms blue on the porcelain plate.
Its groves have vanished, along with one crinkly river,

and since the scene no longer requires a knife
this has dropped nearby like a drawbridge.

The window next to a window we know
must be the princess's. Or so we infer

from the blue curtain and a songbird
who seems to expect a palmful of crumbs.

And that something's amiss—
which is to say, in her story,

it rubs between her shoulder blades
or under one ear as she drifts on

her blue bed. Perhaps it's the insignia
under the plate, "John Cheswick and Sons,

LTD   England///Manhattan,"
that so dismays her. But even

to think this makes the blue castle
shake like a trellis as another pattern

(still blue, now above us)
fills with the grit of unseen stars

ubiquitous, unnumbered, so unlike this plate
hoarding dust and dark in a credenza drawer,

along with an alabastrite bust of a Native
American horseman frozen in full gallop,

and cutlery got at an estate sale in Pontefract.
Where there Cheswicks there or their kin?

Jowly boys with gangly limbs, pale girls
who owned closets full of rococo gowns,

her age but happier in that they are imagined?
Blue castles are surrounded by dry moats

in her story, have no recorded history
save the song she hums in rote distraction

Par dessus nos vertes collines, les montagnes
Au front d'azur, les chaps rayes et les ravines

J'irais d'un vol rapide et sur…
Poulenc's ribald relic passed on

A blue song, scribbled each dusk
into trees that have already gathered

into their own sly clatter two raccoons
who aren't afraid of local, dream-laden children

and a platoon of titmice harrowing an owl
who glides down with one seven-tongued sound.

Maybe he's the hero, not some bungling prowler.
The sea's so dark now it's only a murmur

in elsewhere's throat—or so it seems here,
where empty moats thicken into a pattern of brambles

rounding the edge of the world.
But nothing is safe—not the drawer's teardrop handle,

not the hour, not the drift of song lifting
suddenly, like a blue skirt.

Something more lilting than a boned bodice
lined in jacquards, trimmed by crepe de chine,

Yet less mephitic than chrysanthemums
drooping in cut glass until they shrivel

surely as the suggestion of quirky impropriety
secreted away in the minds of old ladies

who swore never to let such insinuation
besmirch their family name, left delicate plates

instead, blue inked, blue-veined, not meant
for canned carrots, better kept wrapped

in terrycloth, never to expose its verso to the stars.
Only along her long limbs, like the scent of sand

after a hard downpour, had the princess
carried off what the ladies could not speak,

a snippet of song broken off, the dim memory
of a castle, the squared jaw of prototypic

handsomeness animated under her fingertips,
a man who broke horses, mounted carriage wheels,

made his opinions known to the Templar Knights,
spoke softly to dogs when he thought no one saw.

And so what they had been in their world
enters ours, broken by touch,

calling back from leaves curled like fingers
an old sniffer-outer who will drop fragrantly

outside the first junk-shop door.
Plato, hound of the real.

If they're hungry, biscuits and gravy
from white plates in Hunter's Kitchen Cafe

and other doors chiming, loose on their hinges,
even the going-out-of-here-soon's store's,

whose signature goods are already down
to display cases: one waist-high, lit shelf

by shelf, and a taller, revolving one:
$75.00, better money for both.

Here even blue feathers on a stick
(the Candy Castle's owner is dusting

trays in his window) slightly bemuse,
as if summoned from air for a different use,

some other planet's version of reliquary,
a dimension where, were it to exist among

the thumbprints of deep space, they are synchronous
with us, princess and hero, biscuit and gravy,

plate and inscription, two sides of a coin,
the imagined and the real contiguous

and on consignment, smelling of shawl wool and used
appliance. What particles cling to plastic?

What fragments cohere between the blue lines
that turn turret? If the shape of loss

has no shape because it is ongoing, how describe
the way he unfastened her hair from her nape

when both their names, once considered capital,
have washed away, down a crinkly river, vanished?

A whisper is a tendril is the part of her story
she was never told, though she cannot sleep

when black night turns blue with gathering storm—
soon as it bursts, she's out.

Untitled (1958)

Shapes have no direct association with any particular visible experience, but in them one recognizes the principle and passion of organisms.
—Mark Rothko

The proposal: luminous drama.
Ensconced pallor meets an edge
of burnished orange for a shotgun
romance. Share a moment
of horizontal bliss. Then watch
as doubts arise. Ardor turns nasty.
Recriminations grow ever nastier,
spiraling into black, burning coals
of depression, continually brooding

on death. Timelessness passes.
The whole spectrum gets absorbed.
Somehow the couple emerges aglow,
slightly altered, happily lanced
in yellow, each a part of the other
expecting, miraculously to give birth.
When harangued by hue and cry,
they admit to eloping. Step away
from domestic light's embrace

to tally the gradations that hint
at perspective abstracted:
romance, pain, renewal, failure,
the ecstasy of later years, happening
all at once. Step to the surface.
Look there, dead center: the secret
wedding. An exchange of vows
in an effulgent chapel where color
gathers to praise us in our plight.

Along the River of Palms

with Mong Lan

The discordance between thinking and thought
is an illusion—all is a dance that leads you
from the past to the future and the present rolls forever
flat   up/down
a seductive train of our own willpower.
Beside the plastic cow in the miniature railway set,
the tiny man in the peaked cap's facial expression
nearly changes   ages nonetheless
the track looped as the sign for infinity.
Didn't we see that barn before?

Nope.   We've never seen that barn
nor these fields   nor these cows
which moo hopelessly echoing like mirrors
to other cows living in other dimensions
plastic and of the flesh and mooing blood
if it is mooing that we can call that lowing
ruminant mortality. Like the colosseum, the barn
a relic soon to be threshed by vines   in/out
else bulldozed for strip malls to manifest,
new dishes for the feast of the hunter's moon

or the solstice moon of the moon that lows
and bellows the names of all lovers
that suffer and continue to exist
apart in a parallel world
where this world and the other is looped
a Mobius strip infinity
eating its own tail an ouroboros
digesting its own shadow while those relics—
that number scrawled in eyeliner on a napkin,
abalone and antler choker bought from Navajos,
the deck of fading Polaroids of the two of you
held together by a rubber band, shoved in the back
of the closet—decay slowly in half lives
like radioactive isotopes

yes   the two of you rubber-banding
even with the inevitable decay into something
else leading you to think you never existed
the two of you never existed
mere atoms with so much space in between
that you could walk through walls
wormholes into other futures
that never happened except here
the memory of stubble under the tongue
remembered view of an esplanade many stories
above faces postage-stamped to the glass
made one and undone the two of you
mere rivulets along the river of palms

a river of penguins a stream of fierce wind
that makes everything undone
blowing the past away in one clean stroke
white on black and striped over the third eye
the future   empty and patient
filled with the moon on which we live
an alternate reality where all color is washed
away so that every emanation exists as pure
potential   a state of aboutness
in which time salts each body waddling
into and out of burrows in ecstatic display

time limed with salt
and each male body wails
for his counterpart
a rock   under
water and she rises hearing him
responds to his grief-stricken song
with winged vibrations   a ritual dance
ancient as the sound at the center of stars
being born   brightening and dimming
in orbit and oscillation a burst here, a void there,

light seeking light, space the medium of time
until pinprick of awareness grows more glow

the glow of winged vibration glow of a face singed with song
what happens is mere dust
        dust to rise and dusk to finish
the napkin with a lipsticked kiss
is found in her pocket
her fingers twitch over the greasy red evidence
past crumbled into the future desire the arc of a shooting
star blotted in the napkin of the sky
a passageway to where the tongue loses itself
in guttural sound raw and radioactive
shuddered to keening contraction of starlight and dust
in perpetual dance.

Movements

Dance is an art in space and time. The object of the dancer is to obliterate that.
—Merce Cunningham

What an endeavor, nine of you
touring in a VW van, bringing new forms
        of elasticity into being on stages where the crowd,
    if they came at all, would not stay long
          enough to realize they were witness to history
in the dancing, conjunctions
       of chance in music, sets, steps the likes of which
         had never before been choreographed—
Hip jut, asynchronous strut, feline pounce,
      convulsive pirouette, collapses,
  the appearance of notes on a prepared piano
       giving way to silence that was really the sound
of moving feet: women flowing continuously,
    men in spurts, around, together, apart,
           together, in between, over, around,
      with calves stretched, torsos contorted,
        wrists flung out from behind ears like freestyle
   swimmers squeezing every last ounce
         of speed from their long strokes,
           not telling a story,
     but articulating each movement in full
       before falling away, rising into the next instant,
not knowing beforehand how it might feel
        to respond to the music,
    revealing that in costume, on stage, in motion,
      bodies need embody nobody
         save beauty.

Singapore Spring

with Rodger Kamentz

At the pasture for failed seeing-eye dogs
I yipped and rolled in the grass like a puppy
whose pedigreed tail had been shorn to a nib

but whose heart was broken fire from the sun.
How my flesh flared. Erupted to rupture sight,
sunbursts from the dandelions' yellow mind

like the repressed memory of a lion's tooth
dreaming all night inside a feral dog's mind
in seed form, a flux of awareness germinating.

I could no longer play I could no longer play by instinct (1977)

My life at this point is like very old coffeecup sediment.
—Francesca Woodman

Impossible not to retrofit a life into the images.

Knife in motion stays in motion unless acted on by an equal and opposite force.

Wisps of hair from a decapitated head, a hinted-at face, an angel's.

An apparition having more substance than a blinking eye, more presence
than a conversation, imbues an artifact with affect, gesture, complicity.

Themes on variation, like Scarlatti for piano.

Black brocade V-cut gown open to reveal one breast.

Just under the skin's placid surface, tangles of spaghetti, a bubbling over.

Camera a mirror with memory.

In the cleavage a wound, thickly sticky, far past stippled, a soil from which springs a lily
of photo strip: photo booth self portraits, streaked viscous.

How a blade reflects even as it severs.

Tress of white lace draped, just barely, along a dark curtain.

Could be a halo around the body.

We know you threw yourself from the window of a loft in the Lower East Side at the age
of twenty-two, so backwards we project. Forgive us.

When a lesion is self-induced, what lesson induces the self?

Say Breton's "convulsive beauty."

Gaze at the male gaze gazing in discomfort at the supple apple breast puckered into a clue of nipple, a tiny point of light, floating in a pool of its own dismemberment.

The real is constructed, brick by brick. The surreal recalls the trowel.

Gash open the skin. Let ephemera appear.

Frame and Snare Drum

with Tiffany Higgins

Rasp, scrape, reverb, the loop bounce stuttered.
Clasp, gape, perturb, the right atrium mutters
Synaptic stunts to the left atrium, electric shatters
Via iron channels inside the membrane of the cell.

Like cranial nerve ganglia behind an ear cleft
With Bell's palsy or a seashell's self-similar fractal
Whorl shattered by a blind foot, pattern paralyzes
In pieces. I was planning to pulverize
My flesh before anyone else
Could get to it. Shred, pulp, strike
A tat a tat tat from it. Summon
Sutras from striatum. And the common refrain
Takes the form of slow dissolution,
Body threaded into putrefaction, the cells
Rupturing in time into a battery of enzymes
That leave no stain but skeleton to turn
To dust. Rot, crumble, atomize
The once sighted eyes though I can see
No change, even rearranging myself
In simulacrum in front of the mirror.

Yes, we'll end, I nod to him, I
Soothsay to her, but meanwhile
Let's strum this inner anthem,
Let's twitch this awkward manner
On the drum of all regrets
Resynced and repattered as congrats.
It's the pulse of all that lives looped
Back into the soundtrack looming nearer.
Before we could sing, we hummed.

Sounds like Traxx

I can no longer shop happily.
—The Clash (Joe Strummer and Mick Jones)

Before I was all lost in the S*PeRM**K*T,
dubbing the fugitive recyclopedia, or agog
among the penumbras and hungry fatigues,

there was that club with mad pinwheel lights
by the highway off-ramp in DC, an outdoor
strip of beach with towering potted palms

and a volleyball pit/dance floor where rubber
parachute pants morphed in groove to Jesus
Jones and Candy Flip covering the Beatles.

All tuned in, peering over the hedge back then,
those perilous and surreptitious departures
from TamBram family law to gyrating free

time late night with old friends and new punk
rock girls near as the shimmy lasso of hip
would allow, dancing into someone's orbit

then penetrating the periphery, near enough
to touch, to make eye contact, then teasingly
withdraw in bouncing backstep, bass massive

in the ears, the oldest human ritual imagined
fresh as cherry blossom scent at the Navy Yard
in the early nineties. No guaranteed personality.

Emergency Egress and Exits

with Sean Thomas Dougherty

1.
At the bottom of this message I'll paste a number of possible first lines

I'll paste graffiti on turnstiles, overpasses, across the Verrazano straits,
tags the rasp, scrape, reverb, the loop bounce stutter

from the kitchen window, breathing his face (unnamed, utter), a mountain
no one understands, unsung by yak and yodeler.

2.
Overturning a Balinese gong to use as cutting board
in the house of frail, an inexplicable clock. Or the dark adding up hour by hour, note by
broken letter. Thickening into shawls.

3.
Yes, Lycra can improve your performance
stretched across the proverbial wheelbarrow, ruined emblem, but what withers when the
lilacs

lean in the violet light, and you are running toward what

stillness, like the memory of crows gone from the bare olive branches. Years later, you
witness

4.
Burnt-out taxis rust like lozenges on a tongue of rain
City of standing long ago, city of archeological silence?

like the shadows Akhmatova sought,
The discordance between thinking and thought

is absense? Or singing? The dark-haired woman keening,
kneeling at the pasture for failed seeing-eye dogs.

2.

We are always in the space in-between.

—MARINA ABRAMOVIC

The Shanty of Subliminal Governance

with Megan Levad

give me wings
and a wagon wheel for a buckle
and a rattlesnake for a toothpick
and a fastidious mule
my amanuensis
before we set out to explore this new country
of which I have always already been
the final and most fair
emperor
give me wings
and a winking god
with a set of dice
that has more sides than an electron
in a masked ball
of inertial space
a gyroscope that wobbles in place:

take my dictation in loopy script
and longitude in decimal degrees
and dare me to wonder
my peripatetic monk
my monkey, my money, my honey
lazed into mint tea, find x
in relation to me, to the
You Are Here
spot dragged along
beneath us as long
as we have bodies to take
up space: place
a penny on my eyes
to surmise sleep
proffer copper for boat fare
for Charon's obol orbiting
the sacrament of mind looking
back at the slack flesh

with a wish to be two
but not two:

Why Do I Have to Have a Body?
and If I Do, Why Can't I Lie
Back and Enjoy It? This muse, medium
for touch and taste, wily wedding
of muscle and bit to master
and serve pale horse and rider
myth and the tongue to speak it
in eloquent if garbled syntax
a glossolalia of grunt and gesture
believed by Cessationists to be a cloud
of unknowing that shudders
in a frontal lobe lightning storm
of song no errant tremulous jay
can decipher though its fire
still burns the fingertip which longs
to linger longer to feel something
fiercer than flame, a nourishment:

if you feed us
we'll forget how to feed ourselves
but that's the big idea,
making forgetting a function
like the face of the surgeon
upon incision or the cook
lost in a haze of reduction
if we forget you,
we will imagine we planted
the big idea ourselves.

The Tub (1886)

Drawing is not what one sees but what one can make others see.
—Edgar Degas

The mirror on the wall disarms but the face
seen in a basin, scrubbed by hand to remove
the grime of surviving that sediments in streaks
is a truer reflection, not of what we might be
plumed & painted, but who we truly are when
every disguise drops away. *Femme de petite vertu,*
fille en numéro et publique, soumise en maison,
raccrocheuse des boulevards—names not a reason
to suggest the body's more than pliable parlor
meant to house some rich man's brief pleasure,
then be discarded, a filthy rag. Bone-weary,
bent over a tub, washing away a week's worth
of earning bread, sheer animus weighs enough
to drain this fallacy: a fugitive spool of water.

Wanton Textiles

with Reb Livingston

Yes, Lycra can improve your performance
so let's stretch together and recover
that original shape our creases keep
singing about. You are the free-flowing
silhouette and I'm the classic jailer
with a scissor blade deep in my ankle.

Only a few heads are recognizable enough
by their shape to be cut from black paper.
Not former French Minister of Finance
Etienne de Silhouette, whose name
anagrammed is the esteemed in outline.
Not the woman in a beige parka who asks
for everything at the deli counter twice.
Not D.H. Lawrence whose body was buried,
exhumed, cremated, taken by boat to Taos,
else thrown overboard into the Rhone.
What's the greater tribute: an honorary
degree or to be buried in absentia?

These fabrics are slippy situations,
putting us all on the whorepath of snakes
stitching shut the fallen hero figure;
strewn, doom, it's just a flowing skirt
whose hem reaches for sky, for looming
breasts. Are we being set up for greatness
or biblical fall? This ark's no Love Boat.
"Lui Et Elle" is French for "He and It,"
an October surprise is not a golden shower.
It's the difference between Tehran and terrain.

All around the city, mourners hold vigils
in candlelit knots, distribute saffron threads
to barefoot dwellers they will later expunge
from their eyes like cinema on demand.
Does the fact that snatch and achoo lurk

in watch the way nematode does in cinema
mean their pain is not palpable in verse?

Or the inverse: how in covetous fashion
the line mines registers, taps into reservoirs
fed by reading, using genuine suffering
to charge its own brief existence with pies
and pathos, however the trend translates.

Let's rather stretch together, sky, breasts,
silhouettes, our own recognizable heads
unnumbered and damp upon the grass
asking for once, twice, thrice, why count
why wretch, why not bind our thighs around
our pathos and like CBs buzz:

"From here I banish your zipper
and all your senseless buttons.
There are neither worms nor snakes
Between the blades. These are fingers
and a massage, a sublime massage."

Our great religion, like Lawrence's,
is a belief in the blood, not wind
and quibbles flung out like corn to fowl,
not the fine art of backlighting a head,
but giving head backed into a tight spot
illumined by headlights, the grass plush
with dew, contrary to hush in Sunday School,
because the body wants its transport nasty
before it fails, falls into a slough that crooks
the spine, punctuates the veins in relief
upon the calf like a string of ratty Christmas
lights no hose can hide, no leg lifts efface,
but let's try, stretch, recover, uncover, unstitch,
redo, wallpaper with wet tongue, unrepentant
as Mohammed, arms akimbo, surfaces surfed,

caverns craved, a flare of awareness shot
into the sky hotly before ebbing to reflected
sunlight in the atmosphere, dust-smudge
of Zodiacal light, vestigial glimmer shed
by asteroids and comets, moving finger
referred to as false dawn in the Rubáiyát,
like the telsa coils of a bug zapper sparking
orange and blue death to any flier possessed
by insect instinct or ruby-stained pupils,
fluttering. The bandages are ribbons spliced
in swirls of co-eds' auburn manes.

Suture and knots so delicate, so divine,
so gropable, let's purport, let's profess,
let's whitewash the roots to make them
blonde or hazel, zealous and keen. Being
in love with the girl who confuses astrology
with astronomy brings head in the headlights
and mauve walls. Being in love with the boy
who confuses ejection with ejaculation,
organism with orgasm, supernova
with superstition brings swallows, gasps
of astonishment from no huddled crowd.
Yet the idea, once thought, is cast in retrospect
before the time of its doing by nubile rubble
looming vast in the slabyard of recurrent camisoles.

Nothing doing.
Not a single train has left the station
grown over with snarling vetch, sandwich wrappers,
any accordion music long dead to the blown wind
that will still bring snow for a season, remaking
in white what reverts to irrepressible fields
in immeasurable skies, entropy sticky between
girl and boy, itching fabric clinging,
teasing like tassels.

Weaned on such knowledge
the blood can't help but rise to froth the nerves
like the captain his shipmen, whip-crack driven
to reach the green-teeming shore shimmering,
clusters of native women like almonds to unpeel,
to split open lengthwise and eat.

From first tree to blossom, the last fruit harvested
can be juiciest if chosen by a practiced eye.
Where no eyelet halter unravels, stiff
around the clavicle, nothing happens but happens,
slower, less methodical, in tune to undergrowth
brimming with veering air that the girl gulps
too easily with frenzied, practiced, parched mouth,
mist-salted with what she won't acknowledge,
even as she pulls his center out at the root.

She muses, "Why take it in. Why so much?
Will he split me open too? Peal like a bell?
Trade my throbs for a lap dance and silence?
Where is the lather on his lips coming from?"
She doesn't know it's her own engorged
pupils that wills the thin walls to disappear,
disguising the rubble, plying from a paisley-
carpeted motel room a beach at low tide
with dripping knots of nude bathers
licking breeze off wrists and shoulders.

The clumps of refuge, or is it refuse, appear
as artifacts glued together. In short in need
of analysis. She doesn't believe
he's interested in archeology. She thinks
he's sorting the natives from the bathers
chalking up sneers from the well connected.

If a marriage proposal from the captain awaited
answer, there's the key in her locket

to an unused cottage where she could
sob in confidence. Nothing doing.
No end to the drama in sight. Her life out
Jane Eyred Jane Eyre on the way to be locked
in the red room by Bessie: *I resisted all the way:*
a new thing for me...a trifle beside myself;
Or rather OUT of myself...resolved, in my desperation
to go to all lengths.

Scathed, maimed, smitten, scared, struck
with the thought, a dirty murmur of a thought,
that whatever water bathers bathed in
stretched past isthmuses to where her captain captained
surrounded by hairy men, who knew each other
by nickname, knew their vessel as Consolata,
woman made of riggings. Who would lay locked
in bunks groaning with the undulations,
Consolato moving forward in all kinds of weather,
groaning silently into their hands, pretending to sleep,
conjuring faces from childhood villages that diminished
in clarity the further the ship got from shore.

And her captain? Brute as a spiked mace, beating
the docks until the timbers rang with gratefulness.
Being in love with astrology, astronomy, ejection,
ejaculation, not elation full on in the face like the spray
of water dousing a sliding body in a hydrotube.
No reason that any captain could quite articulate.
Why spend so much time on the empurpled seas
away from her? Would he snap back like Lycra
or else rip free? Or would he stretch on, testing
on the strength of her elasticity his entire private
eternity? He might. Some fabrics are meant
to be torn. Sometimes it's easier to refrain,
evade the thought that leaps up like lupine.
Some have quilted miles stitching tight those

dirty murmurs, "THAT didn't come from me!"
A trifle inside themselves, dissolved, searching
for that short cut, that quick snip, that sinking
hip, the bottom of the ocean the mirror image
of a helium balloon released from a child's hand
to snag in a bare oak branch, discreetly.

Reckless, off track, she plead for repair:
Please keep me. Don't tell them where. Hide me.
Fasten me under your undershirt, pressed to your chest,
ruffled in hair. I'm not as indecent as you believe.
I don't knit with disgrace; my wickedness is pure.
I'm in love with something spinning me soft and itchy.

Say we adore our brutes, those we slight and mock.
She and I. Me and her. Odysseus and Penelope.
Rain and holes. Red-eyed tailoresses gnawing
buttons when tongues go wet and laps are climbed
into like thread through a needle's eye.

What he doesn't know is she always finds elation
in ejection, astrology in ejaculation.
From man to woman, from him to her,
captain to captured, friend to fade, you to me,
a skin is stretched so taut it hurts to wear.

It's not scissors straight down the seam,
the flattering A-line shrouding the curves, bulges
that shame us to darkening rooms.
Not the "I have no place else to sleep" line,
the nudge and hush, the deceitful, delightful
"As long as we don't go there" line.

It's what begins at the waist, the round
and dip, the innie and outie, the fabric we rue
that rouses us most.

Sun Wu Kong and Hanuman Share Secrets

with Frances Kai-Hwa Wang

Yes, Lycra can improve your performance but it feels so wrong to be putting on Underarmor with my Hawaiian print skirt for tonight's poetry reading, let alone shoes.

As the leaves change and the first snow falls, I ask myself again, "Why am I here?"

My friends tease that I should turn on the heat, but they all have tenure. Already I feel the chill of the next few months rolling in.

No, you and I should be someplace restless and warm, eating papayas with lime, salt on our lips and sand in our toes.

It is an accident of history that we are here.

A historical accident that we are dropped in an unasked for womb at an unexpected time, languishing on a coast or in the heartland of one continent or another, instead of nestled in a condor's nest.

Leaves turning to fire before they shrivel in the driveway to crunch like pages ripped from old books.

The Buddhists say that each instant our karma is ripening with respect to another, from seeds planted in another life, tended in this one, until the fruit, musky and butterlike in its consistency, with peppery undertones, in its innermost cavity, falls to the ground, begging to be eaten. I would feed you chunks of such fruit if not for the fact of this distance.

Then all you would have to do is follow the trail of lights on this dark night, and walk with me until the moon returns.

It is as simple as clay, mustard oil, wick, and spark.

Artificiere, Firework Drawings (2011)

Each type of machine has a specific movement and produces a specific and unique signature mark.
—Rosemarie Fiore

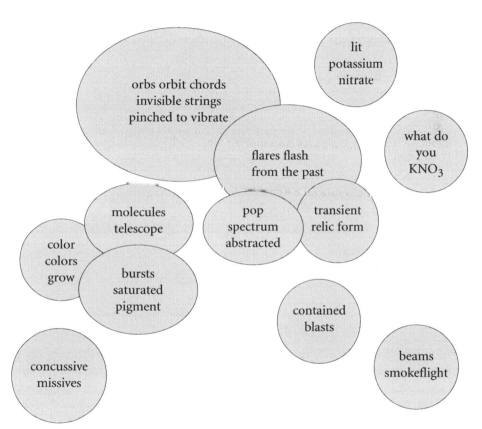

orbs orbit chords
invisible strings
pinched to vibrate

lit
potassium
nitrate

flares flash
from the past

what do
you
KNO_3

molecules
telescope

pop
spectrum
abstracted

transient
relic form

color
colors
grow

bursts
saturated
pigment

contained
blasts

concussive
missives

beams
smokeflight

...a prism beads opaque as a waterdrop's reflection
lit by first burst of light in a curvature of horizon
radiating photonic emission in spectral wavelengths
flaring ions that require dispensation with masks
manipulating canisters filled with molten materials
channeling a sulfuric ballet of chromatic propulsion
spinning carnations / monster balls / magic whips
aka Dr. Faustus or *fumage*–: painting with smoke...

Glass-Bottomed Boat

with Mónica de la Torre

Rasp, scrape, reverb, the loop bounce stuttered
"H-h-ow r-r-r-r-andom is random, it's not even funny."
Overturning a Balinese gong to use as a cutting board,
the contortionist began chopping cilantro for a ceviche to die for.
Yes, Lycra can improve your performance
but try wearing it in bed.
Burnt-out taxis rust like lozenges on a tongue of rain
their plates misleading, is it a 3 or an 8, a 7 or a 9.
This discordance between thinking and thought,
spatter and rot, matter and not.
Slither a tether between top and bottom
and keep your animals in a spruced up farm.
At the pasture for failed seeing-eye dogs
you might find an apt companion.
The castle looms blue upon the porcelain plate
where cumulonimbus clouds make a cameo appearance.
Incursions into the fabric of seawater revealed vitreous lemons
vivacious in spirit, vitriolic by nature.
Turn, hover, bulge like newspaper maché, billow
like bad news on a sunny day.
I know no knot not nautical in nature,
And if you rock the boat you'll end up entangled.

The Escape Ladder (1940)

Monstrous animals and angelic animals.
—Joan Miró

Squiggle-bird beware:
longlegs dangle asterisks
apt to act as parts of traps
when shape meets shape
they colorchange
snooty-nose got a brand
new con & stalk-eyes
about to leave the scene—
it's getting hairy honey
I'd ladder up and out—

Sound Is a Chance Operation

with Vernon Frazer

Rasp, scrape, reverb, the loop bounce stutters
across the gasping urban landscape, its sonic
ambivalence traumatizing hydrant and powerline
with juddering polyrhythms that fluctuate with arrays
of local resonators: pigeons in patterns, airbrake
friction, patter of walkers, a sidewalk drummer
trundling thunder from water jugs, frying pans,
newspaper dispenser, overturned recycling bins.

Dissonance, being a full-time occupation,
plagues the plywood with shadow and seawater,
disrupts the ear with the wind's lifting variations,
an automatic enclosure that deflects the clamor
of each iota that reflects their tonal sequence.

Scratch and scribble, the record rotates, mutates
into a plectrum's call to distance, a quadratic vatic
that echoes gravity's sound in the upper lithosphere
or a pulsation of plausible fossils prior to calcification,
a convergence of spheres thrumming like a tin drum
muffled, a reminder that the scrotal weight of the clock
tower's bells hangs long in a dazzling spray of daylight
bobbing waves, without origin, how amazing grace
has a timbre that cannot penetrate the inner ear.

Chance is a sound operation, proximal to amplitude,
the imperceptible distance between its peak and valley
impossible to harm, the hum volleying with picked
plums and porpoise purpose lacking a mirror-plane.
Hear the Mantra Sastra making mashed potatoes
from our potash music. Hear the banged pot,
the scrubbed dog, the scribbled dish, the botched stitch.
Here the loop bounce flounces in cycles of yugas,
whorls of centuries hurled into the stars headlong.
So long headed nowhere. Where one no longer heads.

Course of Empire (2005)

We're all frozen food for the future.
—Ed Ruscha

Grainy as newsprint, Titian light drawn from capriccios of Venice in decline, else massive neon-incarnadine skies stippled in post-apocalyptic shadow, Rorschach arches an indifferent weight of atmosphere pressed like sfumato in churches or memories of gas stations transformed into mini-markets, then massage parlors, or just abandoned completely, a lamppost and skeletal sycamore where a phone booth once was, landscapes rendered obsolete, indistinct when seen from panoramic vantage points: *anywhere*, anytime from now to the next two hundred years, savage states left mythologized, the pastoral passed over, consummation consumed, drama of destruction and desolation abrogated, even when evolution continues, no progress cycles, the strip malls swarm, try looking at things that normally would be looked through or beyond, like rooftop edges painted with vanishing letterforms, (**Tool & Die**) silhouetted with dead logos ready for the wrecking ball, the (**Tires Trade School Tech-Chem Fat Boy**) shareholders with their brands (**RCA Standard Oil General Foods Compaq Adelphia**) stranded bankrupt.

As Slow As Possible

If something is boring after two minutes, try it for four. If still boring, then eight. Then thirty-two.
Eventually one discovers it is not boring at all.
—John Cage

Heard from a painter how the piece being performed
in a small church in Germany articulates to the history
of the organ, 639 years old in 2001 when the concert
began and scheduled to end in 2640, one note in years.
We were talking about duration in art, how we stop
on a word in a poem or stand in front of a painting
for thirty seconds that could easily be thirty minutes
or thirty years, but how music transpires in time
in a categorically different way, the sound departing
even as it arrives in our ear and nervous system.
This Cage piece is as close as someone could come
to freeing music from temporality, and it commenced
in St. Burchardi church in Halberstadt on what would
have been Cage's 89th birthday and because the score
begins on the rest, it started with a 17-month silence,
save for the sound of the bellows of the instrument
encased in acrylic glass being inflated. Every time
a note changes there's a party and at the last chord-
shift, which will last for 7 years, there were thousands
of visitors, international correspondents and camera
crews, an event broadcast worldwide on a website.
Hyperdurational, said the painter. Only in Germany.

Algorithm, Will You Dance?

with Google Translate

taking all of the potential first lines for collaboration in this order:

Rasp, scrape, reverb, the loop bounce stuttered
Overturning a Balinese gong to use as cutting board
Yes, Lycra can improve your performance
Burnt-out taxis rust like lozenges on a tongue of rain
The discordance between thinking and thought
Slither a tether between top and bottom
At the pasture for failed seeing-eye dogs
The castle looms blue upon the porcelain plate
Incursions into the fabric of the seawater revealed vitreous lemons
Turn, hover, bulge as newspaper mâché, billow
I know no knot not nautical in nature
Graze on the face like a fly on honeydew
Give me wings and a wagon wheel for a belt buckle

then translating into Arabic, then back into English:

Unveil the rear ball using balinisi Coupe
Yes, you can improve performance by Kang-ngalay.
Value for some people in August in a taxi with Rowell Brûlés rhombis.
Considered that the repulsion between the purchase
Is between the head and the bottom of the slide.
Pâturages in dogs
Sex pics, Broder, porcelain blue
Extension when Pietro Eastern blue Groper
Rotates the paper snowman. Besides the Golden nest
I don't know whether the appearance of a windmill.
Before the thief.

then translating into Hungarian, then back into English:

Grated, scrape, reverb, loop skip stutter
Toppling the Balinese gong used as cutting board
For elastic, stretchable performance.

Taxis are spent as Rhombus, rust, the language, the rain
Of thinking and the ever thinking of dissonance
Slides a tether between the top and bottom Margin.
The pasture seeing, eyes dogs successfully:
The Castle looms, the porcelain plate blue
Incursions into the fabric, it turned out, the sea water glass lemon
On the other hand hovers, like a newspaper papier-mâché bulge billows
I know it is not a knot is not its maritime character:
The face as a fly will eat the honeydew.
Give me wings my wagon wheel for we are belt buckles.

      then translating into Haitian Creole, then back into English:

Rasp, justesse, réverbération, the boucle Mate stuttered
Capsize a Balinaise gong to use as Coupé we. Board
Yes, Lycra pants can improve performance you
Burnt-August taxi rouille like rhombes on this band rain
The discordance between live think and that
Slither an attaché between top and bottom
In pâturages for failed dog eyes
The Blue Castle broder on the plaque porcelain
Incursions into the blue de la Mer the vitreux East
Turn, vol, ardennes as mâché newspaper, billow
I am certain that there is no knot not milles the nature
Is over his face as on a thief.
Give me the wings the wagon roues for a boucle waist.

3.

One must still have chaos in oneself to be able
to birth a dancing star.

—FRIEDRICH WILHELM NIETZSCHE

Broca's Area

with Nancy Kuhl

no beveled jewel jagged
rockface cliff edge where
mountain dreams itself
to mist from riverbed
no ancient fault line no
memory of catastrophe
only breath one enters
another departs this is
the perpetual discordance
between thinking and
thought an impossible
figure preserved groove
and catch fixed into flux
fossilized finalized a form
we almost recognize a feather
or bone the skin the shell
the body that intimate shape
like a name or any word
held too long on the tongue

Over the Counter

with Melissa Stein

An exquisite meal lies
upon the porcelain plate
but there is no meal,

no plate, no table,
no wood frame,
no cornerstone.

Only a pinprick of blood,
still teeming in plasma,
not yet russet,

not yet forgotten
by the finger it fell from.
Some kinds of pain

annihilate everything
save origin and throb
crowding the wound.

Other kinds of pain
cannot be indexed
on a 1-to-10 scale

but are more granular,
a keening that takes over
so steadily it resembles

waking and walking.
Whole days given to this.
Years. Natural as breath,

or sex: blessed wish
and ache, fruition,
punishment.

There's no placebo
or panacea, no formulary
pills precisely synthesized

for treatment or cure—
even the tongue
can be bitten.

The Day the Voice Died (1998)

If you possess something but can't give it away, then you don't possess it ... it possesses you.
—Frank Sinatra

It is nearly 1:50 in New York a Thursday
Dante Alighieri and George Lucas's birthday,
anniversary of the day Jamestown was settled,
yes and it is not last call, not in the self-
proclaimed center of the world where the gas
is poured till the slivery moon is closer to light
than dark and I'm boxed in by finks who think
they're big-leaguers when the game's wiffle-ball,
pawing their cell phones and high-fiving,
and wouldn't it have been perfect if Blue Eyes
came on the jukebox and a busload of bobbysoxers
poured in, but no, this is real life, 1998
                                    and I'm holding
a watered-down vodka tonic in a haze of smoke,
and there're no screws wearing suits with fabric
finer in the lining than upon slim lapels, no crooning,
no louche swagger or clacking of billiard balls,
hardly no one carrying a Zippo and a roll of dimes,
and I will finish my drink, walk down the Avenue
of the Americas to the A/C/E line running local,
moving slower than I should, in synchronicity
with cabs idling curbside and across the Hudson,
Hoboken, which I can't see, glittering languidly,
one might even say, except for this fact of real life,
in a pose of mourning, pouring wave after wave
of brass and bel canto from here to eternity.

Desert Math

with Louis Bourgeois

The discordance between
thinking and thought

has made cold the inadequacies
of our most profound philosophies

have given rise to death and life
simultaneously

even structurally, the way rot
couches in seed

like a script that provides
conditional instructions

to delete itself after a given
span of time

becomes itself a double-negative
in an expansive

fatigue, voiding
within a void

the source of everything
even as it is just hypothesized,

traced back to a point in time
so heavy there was only space,

not the pluses
of cacti in an unsolvable

equation of sand.

Two Water Towers Red (2008)

...a sliver of light hitting the street at an angle...
—Sonya Sklaroff

       as   in
      what   dusk
      passes through
how the weight of the not-yet-night-sky upon the rooftops
pushes down upon the thrust of cornice and spire, the light
interpenetrates   ochers like red clay   dug out from
loam with hand   axe or mattock yet   is the reverse
of earth being firmament, not firm but atmospheric, some-
how invisible from the sidewalks most of the time walkers
walk by with their dogs on a leash or their ears plugged up
with music then   suddenly, up ahead   everything lit
up with bonfire   you can never think   how you did
not notice before. Think Toni Morrison in Jazz describing
the citysky emptying itself of surface, "more like the ocean
than the ocean itself," so close you could pluck it, a peach
made of scattered light, fine particles born from interstellar
collisions, while   the deepening glow   grows redder
in dream-space   exhuming a buried   rhythm beat
from footfall, taxis, curling stream, pigeons, the shuttered
windows flickering with television, fluctuating in shadow
as bodies pass by, all of it rising up and up to meet what's
falling, pulled earthwards by gravity until an equilibrium
so ephemeral it cannot last longer than minutes arrives to
stretch boundless light: the whole city as living organism

New York City (1942)

...the metropolis as the embodiment of abstract life...
—Piet Mondrian

Grids map Manhattan: thin spires of skyscrapers
patterning the skyline, distended accordions
connecting certain extra-long buses, interlaced
steel trash cans, architraves around doors, flags
on poles, avenues four blocks long perpendicular
to numbered streets headed crosstown, rooftops
      like a
      column
      of graph
      paper,
      windows
      lit up,
sidewalks seamed, manhole covers crisscrossed,
confessionals, peep show booths, teller windows,
rows of brownstones, crosswalks walked across,
Central Park's green quadrangle, hotdog cart's
checkered grill an engraver's mold, TV antenna,
      subway
      rails,
      bridges
      across
      the East
      River
from ferry-deck, metal grates pulled down over
storefronts, all symmetry excluded, police car's
flashing lights, chain-link fences, strips of benches
like weave of fabric, concatenation of parked cars,
            plinth
            of the
            globe
            in front
            of the
            Trump
            Towers,

billboards jutting from Times Square, stock ticker
ticking in the window of an equities firm, checks
on the gingham skirt the secretary wears, elevators
rising, trees potted equidistant, fingers on guitar
        strings,
        news-
        papers
tied up in stacks, hemlines that create the living
rhythm, crosses atop cathedrals, computer screens
in cubicles, steel girders hooked by cranes, spines
on a book vendor's table, bacon strips on hot plates,
latticed sewer grates, networks of lines interlocked.

A Square of Blue Infinity

The true adventurer goes forth aimless and uncalculating to meet and greet unknown fate.
—O. Henry

Snookered by traffic lights that turn
the swim up 9 into a knot,
Middletown's fringe tediously damp
with the same almost-wet that streaks

the windshields in such a way
that wipers twitch ineffectively
against the hard light, clear edges,
what Pound claimed no democratized

campaign could maintain stages
its revival upon the smudged glass
morning. Red stutter of brake lights.
Wide world winnowed to a stretch

of road from the coast to Hartford,
my passage sealed from traffic
and saturated with felicitous diction,
the glories of books on tape,

dear sir, your stories spoken by
a second-rate thespian for whom
even commercials have dried up.
Nearly a century since you hopped

a freighter into the banana boom,
wanted by the feds for bank fraud,
just another *gringo* in Honduras
with a scar the source of which

he'd rather not reveal over mojitos.
did prison teach you the difference
between prosaic and prosodic
prose or was it being fêted

in the streets of the city you died in as
"Caliph of Bhagdad-by-the-Subway,"
most colorful newspaperman in the five
boroughs? You'd work all winter

on fifths of scotch while editors
screamed for copy, putting down
the occasional yarn on a typewriter
missing a few keys. You outwitted it

by using a period for an apostrophe.
Somewhere pent in your small flat,
hunched over an overflowing ashtray,
memories of endless, rolling Prairie

must have uncharted the city's grid,
leaving you a brief glimpse
into something so large that no one
could ever belong to or even trace

its terrible shape, though you tried
with sinuously wound sentences
laden with polysyllables, brogue,
and what became a characteristic

plot twist. I've heard your critics
complain that you're too mannered,
your phraseology ostentatious,
your enduring reputation as a hack,

but what art rebuffs contrivance?
Even the trees flaming into autumn
north of Middletown *look* different
to each of the passing drivers

and are something altogether other,
like your stately delineations
that run from the "hectic, haggard
perfunctory welcome like the specious

smile of a demirep" to "a polychromatic
rug like some brilliant-flowered,
rectangular, tropical islet surrounded
by a billowy sea of soiled matting"

all in the course of the same story,
one that is not believable, true,
but not meant to be, any more
than Sophocles intended Oedipus

Rex to be a literal transcription
of a typical Athenian nobleman's
quirky yet predestined misfortune.
No, you are like the conductor

of a Viennese waltz, peering
past your gloves as the orchestra
swells, as a gentleman in tails
bows low above his lady's hand,

lips poised above but never making
contact with her niveous flesh,
proving that between a thought
and its realization, space is infinite.

In your world, the wrong man
gets the right job, bums who want
to be arrested can't, while rich
misers receive sudden comeuppance.

you and I both know it's akin
to dance, not cartography,
analogy, not mimetic affirmation,
that the trajectory of no life

could so gracefully arc toward
a spindle of fate, abruptly changing
direction. Unless of course we take
yours: frail North Carolina

ex-con who rose to international
literary renown in less than nine years,
then died in a New York hospital,
penniless, drunk, and alone, uttering

last words that one of his own
characters might have spoken:
"Turn up the lights, I don't want
to go home in the dark."

From where I'm sitting,
there is no dark, the whole sky
is lit up like a stadium, a thick braid
of traffic forms then unravels,

the Cisco Kid has just traversed
an arroyo to find his cheating lover,
and next to me a gaunt woman mouths
lyrics, slowly, to a song I cannot hear.

Love and Decay

with Harriet Levin

Graze on the face like a fly on honeydew,
bend over toward someone so that your entire body alights
imperceptibly, on the cusp of action, afternoon fretted
in long lines of light through a near-drawn shade.
Between what you do and what you don't do, what you can't
(but could) or haven't (again) but have imagined,
fates hang suspended in the whirl of motes
over sugar, over a piece of fruit, over an orb
smashed on the ground. The bride walked out
of church with her bouquet, then seeing it
still in her hand, she dropped it. The airplane running low
on fuel cannot circle back. Hear its continual roar.
Then reconsider the buzz of a fly viewed from below.
Or try the fly-by buzz of reconsideration, the rush
of remembering the alighted-upon body, wing and engine
too close to sun to cast a shadow. Before banking
hard toward any strip of land or water, the moist interior
of fruit cannot be inferred. Not even on radar.
The interior is always hidden in folds.
Skin is never tell-tale, only an obstruction, as in flight,
something to go around. So much to discard, to peel away.
What if there are wormholes, brown spots, bruises?
And because of this chance, because a honeydew
left out in sun will eventually seethe with maggots,
its brain-skin teeming until its folds disappear
in a blizzard of winged consumption fresh from a puparium
grown beneath a dirt clod, one of a few hundred eggs
laid at once to lap up sap with fleshy mouthpart?
Say as infant who didn't have an appetite, no bloated
stomach most desirous of the lush
sweetness of juice? Not only juice. Sun, wind, motion.
That it started with rocking and always being carried.
There was no difference then between those arms
and one's own, so that the earth was perceived
as one body, all in motion, an entire swarm

circling, warmth more tidal than a Ferris wheel.
This was before in a mirror, reflection stared
back at you in a kind of dare, before you worried
you might break the honeycomb of your disappointments
against the bark of your mother's breastless back
but did nothing instead, hiding away with flyswatter in the hamper.
This mirror, its flat glass in which everything is seen
in reverse—remember how the carney stopped the Ferris wheel
and we rocked up there a spinning cage,
then lurched forward in the skipped beat—into the quiet
of a room of no birds, not even a shadow
of a muscle gone slack or the torn limb of a tree branch,
sprung from reaching.

Untitled (PH-58) (1951)

…with tense slashes and a few thrusts the beautiful white fields receive their color…
—Clyfford Still

Matte black a palimpsest for paintings	/ paintings
violated by public exposure, reclaimed	/ reclaimed
through concealment in lustrous soot	/ in
a fragile red line blooms through, scar	/ fragile
of awareness overwhelmed by space	/ awareness
touched gray, just in the left corner—	/ just touched—
never more than pigment on canvas,	/ canvas
the way a leaf is vein and ridge prior	/ is
to symbol, to taxonomy, to the terms	/ to
which camouflage apoplexy as animation,	/ camouflage
even to write these lines is an act	/ lines
of betrayal, leaves a bloodlike trickle.	/ of leaves

Architect Attacked by a Goshawk, or the Unsilent Night

It comes from everywhere and at the same time you can't pinpoint where any of it is coming from.
—Phil Kline

Turns out there's an aggressive bird in the woods
by the farthest studio that must have just given birth,
because it's patrolling the treetops for intruders,
like artists from Brooklyn sauntering to glimpse
ferns & deer scat, unaware that mama will swoop
like a scythe at their head & in the case of the architect,
draw blood from his scalp. When he tells the story
at dinner, he's surprisingly calm though the evocation
of the rasp of talons sends shudders through half
the table. Wear a helmet next time, someone brays.
Wave a stick, someone else proffers. I want to go
on a hawk-walk, mourns another, nothing ever happens
to me. Come to Atlanta in December, says the composer,
& you too can be part of something cool. He describes
putting on Phil Kline's ambient auditory perambulation
caroling tour through the streets, participants
carrying boom boxes and amplifiers that play one
of four different parts that interact with each other
as they walk through the city, New York City originally,
going from Washington Square Park to Tomkins Square,
but now transposed to cities all over the world.
Something about the swirling sounds, chimes
& warbling bells, reflecting off buildings, into open
spaces, intermingling with street noise as the sound
moves through a mapped route, always the same
yet different every year, in each new place the piece
is performed, recaptures the physical mystery
of inhabiting place by moving through it,
leaving like a wisp of smoke an ephemeral trail
of reverberations that receding into memory
takes on the aural dimensions of the sublime.
At a nearby table, the architect is touching
the back of his head & saying that fucking hawk.

The Castle Looms Blue

with Joseph Stanton

1.
The castle looms blue upon the porcelain plate.
A boat—blue, too—sails off-shore,
sinister in its whisper of winds,
while the beautiful daughter and her furtive lover
cross the blue bridge in the porcelain rain
and embrace under the blue willow.

When they look up from their passion
two gigantic birds,
ridiculous in their unlikely warp of wing,
have filled most of the glazed white of the sky
with a verve décoratif.

By the time you have finished
eating the last of the crumbs off the plate
the lovers have achieved their blue consummation,
devoutly, behind the porcelain temple
and sailed off in the blue boat,

while two men—
a wealthy suitor and the girl's father—
watch in azure silence on the pale bridge
as ceramic willow leaves
fall and fall.

2.
Not unlike the snowflakes that settle in drifts,
plowed and salted brown, in Detroit
which has just gone bankrupt, where a couple,
newly married, unpack their belongings
from crates that once held Guatemalan oranges.

Under a framed playbill, a crumpled cat mask,
plaid scarfs and a stack of 45s—Rare Earth,

The Marvelettes, The Contours—the daughter
now turned wife drew from tissue
the very plate that embraced edges of so many knives,

a twisting genetic line of your forbearers,
men with moustaches or stern women in high
collars, whose sketchy sepia-toned photos
you may or may not once have seen.
Here she is, fingering the scalloped edge,

with a lacquered thumb tracing the orifice
like inside a shell found at a beach where boats
dot the horizon and enormous seagulls
dive for bluish bits of trash.
By the time you ever crumble a croissant
on the plate, she too will have disappeared.

3.
Because it is Friday night she has placed
their two best plates—
hers with its delicate decoration in blue,
his with its precise red-brown trim—
on the counter of their tiny kitchenette
ready to receive the meal she has prepared,

but her husband, just home from work,
remains oblivious to her pleas
and sits, still in his work attire—
white shirt, black vest, and blue tie.

He is hunched over his newspaper
as if the scores inked on the page
were the reason for his life
within this tight parenthesis
of yellow walls,

where his wife now sits, too,
luminous in her red dress.
She has stopped insisting
and sits by the piano,
plunking the same key
over and over again, a D-sharp

that Edward Hopper can't hear,
staring at the couple from his seat
on the elevated train
sketching them quickly
for a painting he might want to do,

and the wife,
distracted by the rumblings of the train,
begins to pick out the melody of "Ain't We Got Fun"
and thinks about her blue plate
and how she would like to cruise
away anywhere under its fragile sails.

4.
Not a tableau of a happy chappy
with a hippy whooty, as the dropouts
on the corner contend, snapping
their fingers and beat-boxing freestyle
riffs that contrast with their riches,

or lack thereof, only one of them
ever even having eaten off a real plate.
They band together to shoot dice,
play stoop ball and skully with bottle

caps, anything to waste the hour
before they know they must return
to their women or to a whirlpool

of viscerally swirling downward
addiction to the bottle or syringe.

The most exact possible transcription
of intimate natural impression,
what Hopper was after in painting
those solitary figures in shadow,
might better need cornet and drums,

music instead of paint to capture
the sheer desperate, frenetic, bluesy
hustle of life in the projects, where a boat
is but a shape on the screen, a piano
only something to hear struck in a pew.

5.
Sometimes I was along for the ride
as he ran his Debit.
Later we would veer over to Forest Park
to fish tight-line off the side of a blue boat.

A castle abandoned after a World's Fair
loomed blue on the horizon,
its ramparts catching
late afternoon light.

Our lines would sing
every little melody of current,
refrain of rock, delicate trill of fish nibble.
It was a tune the string made
against the unmoving finger;
the instrument playing its soloist.

With finger on string we could feel
to the depths of watery places.

We could sit for hours,
catching little
beyond glimpsed landscapes.
Sometimes he only watched the line,

but I liked to rest my finger on the string
so I could gaze at the other boats
or the deft red-winged blackbirds
and their awkward young
zig-zigging tight lines
from ground to sky to tree.

We spoke no more
than did the water or the clouds
drifting in the breeze.

6.
Glimpsed in flashes off the highway, a medieval jawbone
sketch of crags against the skyline, then river between trees

and car, car, car as usual. Early mornings, alone with radio,
you drive this stretch, and on some days startle at the sudden

vista of another century, the conjuration of arrow loops,
crenellations, machicolations and murder holes, a barbarism

that on closer inspection reveals itself to be a simulation
of the medieval, the quirky former residence of the stage actor

who brought the deerstalker cap, tweed Inverness cape
and Calabash pipe to Sherlock Holmes. Sir William Gillette

who designed a fieldstone home in the German Rhineland-
style, a gnarled knuckle of a mansion that allowed him to spy

on his guests with elaborate mirrors, escape through trick
doors, and ride a train with guests like Charlie Chaplin around

his estate. The Nutmeg State is full of estates thinking nautical
thoughts of birds and yachts upon the Sound, but the inner

cities of Hartford, Bridgeport, and New Haven stay parched
places, bereft of porcelain plates and bobbing blue boats.

When Gillette died, without an heir, he precluded possession
of his land by any "blithering sap-head who has no conception

of where he is or with what surrounded." You must confess
then to having no clue about what special form of depthlessness

and difference this drive each morning passes you through,
where you can see castles and panhandlers mere minutes apart,

where the Connecticut River swells from Quebec to Long Island,
and where, at the end of the day, you will start it all over again.

7.
At night it seemed a house in dark, fairytale woods
so high were the maples and oaks in every yard.

By day it was just another suburb
wedged between railroad tracks and expressways,
paths of desperate transit to the desperate city,
desperately needed because Long Island is so long.

But most nights blue napkins rested on a rosewood table,
and we ate off the good china with your ancient, Irish mother
who loved the color blue so much that you made sure
the walls of her room and all its furnishings remained
in that rarest of colors even decades after her passing.

So hard now to remember you
and your red hair,
and those ornate plates, so long gone, too.

8.
Wisps spilling from a passel,
floating spirits in the form of flickering lights
in the evening sky just barely visible
beyond the curtain's lace edge
stained a faint lentil bean color.

The alcazar of the stars serrates depth
with waves particulate as sand-grains
if impossible to hold in the hand.
Sounds an open palm might make
passing through the twilight air.

However we happened here, forged
from reptile, neuron and pure want,
vaster realms populate space beyond us,
the castle a plate to eat forms from,
full of conjecture plum-ripened in the sun.

Inquisition Palace and Jewish Ghetto, Lisbon (2009)

…human and ecological echoes at places fractured by trauma and political violence…
—Quintan Ana Wikswo

scarred door-frames retain
       suggestion of gouging
nothing specific the way
       clouds form from rising
air cooling to shape-shift
       how earthquakes raze
buildings that are built again:

       take amnesiac Rossio Square,
           where waves of black
       & white cobblestones verge
           a mineral homage
       based on the sea yet geometric
           no trace of the quarry
       work performed by lost fingers:

       now flashpackers unfold maps
           buskers reel sing & jig
       vendors roast chestnuts
           laminate photos for tourists
       new surfaces to varnish the past
           with a translucent eternal
       present again & again reborn:

       on café tables heaped high
           with bowls of snails
       salgados pastries agua com gas
           in baroque pediments
       shadows under conical pinnacles
           the columns twisting
       like rope strands or human hair:

       overlay upon overlay if palimpsest
           clouds retain carbonaceous

memories of the city's many Jews
          burned at this very spot in space
no eulogy falls nor plaque raised
          the flower stalls still burst
with bunches of fresh lavender:

encoded in bygone yellow facades
          dripping with hieroglyphs of laundry
lost hands begin to dismantle the bronze
          statue of Dom Pedro IV
turning his patina back into slurry
          cries from the last auto-da-fes
resounding once more for all to hear:

only in hearing such scorched song
          may old scars unmar unmark
mezuzot reappear on doorposts
          red-tiled roofs reaching back
through time by the rushing banks
          of the *Tagus* to find a place
recollected unconverted & gestational:

The Theory of Radioactivity

with Brian Turner

Burnt-out taxis rest like lozenges on a tongue of rain
in Phnom Penh, where the suctioned geckos stare for hours
at the zigzag tiles of the *Commissariat's* roof, double zeros
doubled back in pools spooled around sandstone fingers
pointed at the past life of stars, the ornately carved prangs
of Angkorian temples clenching open a cool space to pray
under distant frigate birds that ride among streets of clouds,
their wings in a tropospheric heat as Bikini Atoll
lifts the year 1952 in a column of ash, snow
of calcite and coral to follow, the drift and falling
chunks of archipelago vaporizing into thin air
on eternal patrol with vague whispery outlines of hands
that anchored an array of destroyers, a show of strength.
Now the coconuts on palms still suffused with cesium
glow faintly at night like phosphorescent bowling balls
or the eyes of sailfish and skipjacks once hooked
and pulled hard through the blue current of eternity,
as we all are and will be, our ears filling with white
noise like a purely theoretical construction, a solar flare
that ejects through space ions of unknowable unknowing.

Tempo Rubato Luminoso con Moto, or, Notes from The Field Guide of Postlapsarian Instruction

with Lisa Russ Spaar

The woodpecker's catechism, doctrinal, drilling the house,
is the discordance between thinking and thought,
is the candelabra of your hand, there, effacing thought,
is the clock's cluck-clucking: *What is the chief end of man?*
Like egg whites into batter, each mammal brain furrowing
folds in layers better to fit the fetal growth—rapid, bastular—
leaving petroglyphs of spidery, chromosomal pictograms
abraded deep into grooved walls for your someday
senescent mind to decipher. Please, your hand again.
There. There, there. Another furrow of knowing.
What rule hath God given to direct us? Inklings, and so forth.

O, pileated hammerer of post, oak, rood,
making feast of this attic dormer, *what reason have you
for saying so?* Seconds eat seconds from your palm,
another grain in the sand mandala the wind whisks,
itself whittled raw by such unseen imminence
that each shape pours from a glass to be absorbed.
A: *You shall have no other gods.* Q: *What does this mean?*
I have seen your body pendant with eon.
The desire-devoured story; the roof given wings.
There. Not there. Like silt and ash from consideration
of fire, on fingertips the catechesis of the fossil bed.

Route 66 Motels (1973)

balance, wonder, luminosity, method and clarity are under the same sky as satire, failure, ignorance and fear
—John Schott

Over a half-century since The Grapes of Wrath named the "Mother Road" escape route from the Dust Bowl to the Gold Mine of California, just decades since Nat King Cole got his kicks on Bobby Troupe's song, but in these flattened black-and-white contours of stucco haciendas and concrete teepees sprouting T.V. antennas, there's a chord of loneliness shivering the fretboard of a lost America: vacant if neon, shrunk down still vast in loneliness, replicated in rooms identically shuttered, a land of wiry telephone poles, tractor-trailer cabs and a folding plastic patio chair, unsat upon, shot through bellows of a Dierdoff 8 x 10, no longer manufactured.

Savagery

with Eileen Myles

The castle looms blue
upon the porcelain plate
soon it began quacking,
quivering like perpetually-
in-motion Jell-O, all hue
and rainbow jiggle.
All spinning like tops.
Inside was another story how
ever. Moths fought,
Protein-packed
flagrant little paper
weights using head
lights for celestial
navigation.

The Virtues of Vandalism

with Daniel Donaghy

Burnt-out taxis rust, lozenges on a tongue of rain.
      We hurl rocks against doors and fenders,
smash through windows, kick tires axle-deep in mud.

We hop onto running boards and yell *Follow that car!*
      We jump from trunk to rooftop to hood
over a hundred top lights, over ferns, puddles, rising moss.

We have all day. The cars sink too slowly into forest
      floor, so we make up for lost time
by hastening decay, leaving boot prints on hoods

we traverse, unscrewing gearshift knobs to hang
      as hip hop medallions around our necks.
Soon, the underbrush will overwhelm these chassis

and we'll have to shave, but for now, nothing exists
      but these still odometers and the stories
we steal from their miles, these fused steering

wheels on which we tap time with our fists,
      tuning long-gone radio dials to whatever
song we want, bad asses, OGs, mountain kings,

spit-screaming rhymes into each other's grills,
      scratching bass grooves into dashboards
far from home, far from school's dead engine

of fractions and film strips and allegiances
      we learned by rote, far from corner
girls we conjured up and advised to hang on

in our battered back seats, calling out the moon
      to echo with our brazen sound, shine
pearlescent off the chrome drop top of dope rides

just like this, but in perpetual motion, throaty
            rumbling from drive into overlook,
any quick escape from the fumes of family

we choke on like the one among us huffing
            Krylon Gold Metallic from a cut
off sweatshirt arm because he will always be

there to push it too far. There's pure potential
            in a windshield before it smashes.
A funhouse mirror image of grace in that sliver

of night where it seems like anything can happen
            to anyone at anytime and we are flying
smack dab through the middle of that energy field.

The Two Fridas (1939)

wave - ray – earth- red - I am.
—Frida Kahlo

corseted heart
raison d'être et de souffrir
through the veins of air
a twined system of tubes
convalescent songs
snakes unembroidered feather
under bronze skin paling
        turquoise *retablos*

how red corridos sound
miracle that courses
through stuccoed adobes
transparent as buried ice
sunken Tehuana
bone-dry blizzards
watery lips slightly pursed
brandied blood

    Diego
      Diego
      snip

        snip

         snip

once a loosed rod slashed
gold flake patina wafted
no sufficient bandage
left body bent immobile
the shape of glacial patience
that has no explicable scrim
but convulsive vibrations
not sick but broken
in voluptuous transience
a syringe or ferrule or nipple
strings of bone torn
hand in hand until the end
leaving the flesh joyful

drill bit to pierce skin
from a fractured package
mujer tan cansada
bundled alone in blue house
birthing a disembodied eye
no unexposed surface
skies mottled with storm
a taint stained yellow
a brush dreams of being
the self other than itself
cleaved by a knife in two
appears shimmering in air
never, never to return—

The Third of May (1814)

It is not easy to retrain the instantaneous and transitory design that issues from the imagination.
—Francisco De José Y Lucientes

When they come for you, Cossack-capped,
in lockstep, carrying the black eye of death
against their shoulders, how will you react?
Bending low, earthward, hands interlaced
in supplication, eyes pleading for mercy
from the uniforms striding toward you,
or brandishing a fist, jaw clenched,
resolute with bright inflections of hatred?
With your face deep in your hands, blinded,
telling yourself *this can't be happening,*
no, my life was not meant to end like this,
or hiding behind someone, anyone, hoping
that somehow you're missed, that they run
out of ammo, that your neighbor will take
the bullet meant for you and you'll escape?
Or will you fling out your arms like a father
receiving his son home from traveling abroad,
elated to know an end to all journeying?

The Perils of Homecoming

with Priya Sarukkai Chabria

The castle looms blue upon the porcelain plate,
the shepherdess rests within the coffee cup's gilt,
palm-sized Pierrot sits Pierrette on his knee for a kiss
her ceramic tutu ruffled by his haste while inches
away The Pied Piper leads his rats of silvery clay:
this menagerie once within memory's chamfered glass
bolts, for pain's insoluble grains gargle up the throat
in an inverse pantomime of tongue and tract. Such flow
of grief cannot be digested or broken down by bile
but persists moment after lifetime after era,
an inheritance of malady the mask of which a pale
face wears as persuasively as the ochre, the dead
as inexorably as the unborn. Alas! The Cumaean sibyl
peers (more granules than limbs) from her bell
jar on the shelf and whispers I want to die!
weighted by knowledge's intractable metamorphoses
into light as the body shrinks. Around
her ampulla glitter shards of promises, illusions
lost, broken rings of love , the salver of desire
beyond salvaged. Yet all's not lost, perhaps. Aren't
all dichotomies birthed from a whole? Squint.
Unpeel eyes. Flurry the dust. What's
that burning, burning, burning, burning sensation
like the smashed-up bits of asteroids and comets
orbiting a planet to retrace a path hewn from prophecy
in a self-reflexive knot or biofeedback loop. Circulatory
ouroboros of eternal return where a serpent eats its own
tail. Just so, each of us a gravitational body around
which our past rotates--faces of lovers, shards of toys
we once imagined alive, the cave of a hundred
openings where songs take the shape of oak leaves,
where we may have played in this or that lifetime,
and where we may yet play again.
Yet the cool smoothness of porcelain,
the grains of gold gilt beneath blind fingertips, the dust
on Pierrette's net tutu of glass that shadows touch —what's
this lust that burns into bones, what's this we cannot

turn back on, tail in our mouths, we who are toys
of eternal return? What's this grief, this wonder, this
mesh of clay, colour, fire that constructs our glass, this
brokenness that bleeds prayer?

Last Turn on the Left

with Clare Rossini

Yes, Lycra can improve your performance
but that little red sports car, only its music could tell you where it's off to,
a vineyard in the foothills, a Rosh Hashanah Seder, or a cliff's edge,
its mids and woofers growling with guitar or languid with opera.
And when you get to where you thought your thought was leading you,
that note-smeared testament nobody can pin to a latitude
you'll find the excrement of grief, its uncontrolled movement
of leave-taking, every arrival latent with its own departure,
like the Buddhist sutra on the mindfulness of the body in decay
sung by ancient Indian pilgrims in the charnel grounds
where a corpse still green, still held together by sinew,
becomes the bespattered subject of contemplation
Where does an hour go? Same place as a life. I
thought I was following this wending road toward the sea's
terminal blues, thought the heart was taking me there
by its weight and chill. I thought I was being led.

Funk & Wag: Revivals to Schopenhauer (2012)

The survival of my own ideas may not be as important as a condition I might create for others' ideas to be realized.
—Mel Chin

1.

Play that Romulus like a ring-billed gull sculls	= play
for fish, focused, plucking those she-wolf teats	= fish
like saxophone keys until the Sabine women,	= like
seized, bleat & drag their bare feet for pleasure	= pleasure
that resembles terror the closer they come,	= terror
the closer they come. Resignation, roundheads,	= resignation
is Schopenhauer's supreme wisdom, all impulse,	= wisdom
pulse & palsy, *rouge et noir* played until *refait,*	= until
until Saturn's rings are rung with Ramses' ring	= rings
& the finger candy of a Frankish king a beaver	= Finger
will pilfer to weave his dream dam like a prayer	= prayer
rug trimmed with tread like a block of rubber	= tread
sliced for tire stock, another polymer vulcanized	= another
for profit. Cut & paste to accrue & negate context.	= negate
Channel the indefinite multiplicity of the material	= indefinite
& immaterial world for to stand still is to petrify.	= still
Even words veer across the page trailing a dust	= words
tail of histories that hide in interstices between	= hide
letters. From Rochester to Saratov, Saarbrücken	= letters
to Santiago, Rome to Ruanda-Urundi or Saipan	= to
to Rhodesia, the great books necessarily dissemble.	= books
Rather present a partial perspective that torn out	= perspective
& reimagined can be seen again, gathered in form,	= form
modulated to order, placed & reconfigured, shaped	= to
to less provincial taxonomy through the processes	= through
of sanitary engineering, fused into hybrids of life.	= fused
Juxtapose, then, flow of space over time until new	= new
performances, which while familiar resemble nothing	= nothing
ever before experienced, can occur: a collective self-	= self
portrait with flags & machines; a miscegenation	= portrait
of bird & insect fashioning an illegible glyph;	= illegible
a rabbit with ribcage antlers for ears; a garland	= with

of icons of unknown origin; cracked, androgynous   = unknown
busts basted back together so gender is rendered   = rendered
archaic; renowned mouths of mouthpieces muted   = muted
into a frozen wave a single sailboat like a rock   = wave
sits silently upon; a bridge traversing dimensions   = dimensions
of wealth from arid tableland to azure coast;   = arid
natives at the well & man as the root of the tree.   = the
Cue up the zany *vidushakas* to slapstick & parody   = cue
the royal court with thick makeup, simian beards   = the
& Sanskrit barbs. Sprinkle in a few schnausers   = barbs
snacking on shit-dwelling scarab beetles & shade   = shade
the silky salukis with sails so they can't see or smell = the
the noxious cloverleaves exploding the sacred   = exploding
into a storm of shrapnel that once fragmented   = shrapnel
will forever remain in fragments: continents adrift   = forever
in rising water, shards of phenomenon arising   = shards
from the universal will's irrational, embryological   = irrational
energy where the body is an idea & the punch line   = body
of the cosmic joke is simply that God is a gun.   = the

2.

The body, irrational, shards forever.   = forever
Shrapnel exploding the shade barbs   = exploding
the cue. The arid dimensions wave,   = dimensions
muted, rendered unknown with illegible   = unknown
portrait. Self nothing new, fused through   = new
to form perspective. Books to letters hide   = form
words still indefinite, negate another tread   = words
prayer. Finger rings until wisdom,   = until
resignation, terror, pleasure, like fish play.   = play

3.

Play until words form new unknown dimensions exploding forever.

PROCESS NOTE

Each of the collaborative poems in this collection was written in response to the potential first lines indicated in the poem "Algorithm, Will you Dance?" I sent this list initially to the poets with whom I collaborated, and they added to it, sometimes in the mail, but more frequently over email. They sent their additions back to me, and I appended to what they had added, bending and revising the work as we proceeded. When we reached an appropriate stopping point, we each took turns revising the final poem until it emerged in its final state. Though that description is reductive: since each act of collaboration was significantly different and unique, I tried to take my cue from the inclination of the poet I was working with and feel that our mutual attention was surprising. We discovered where the poem wanted to go by going, often channelling a third voice, neither mine nor my collaborator's, but a spirit birthed of lyric that seemed almost magically to materialize

Abundant gratitude to the following poets who were willing to embark upon this improvisational jam session:

Louis Bourgeois, Priya Sarukkai Chabria, Jim Daniels, Mónica de la Torre, Daniel Donaghy, Sean Thomas Dougherty, Camille Dungy, Vernon Frazer, Google Translate, Tiffany Higgins, Frances Kwa-Hwang Wang, Rodger Kamenetz, Lena Kallergi, Nancy Kuhl, Mong Lan, Megan Levad, Harriet Levin, Reb Livingston, Eileen Myles, Alvin Pang, Melissa Stein, Brian Turner, Clare Rossini, Lisa Russ Spaar, Joseph Stanton and Terri Witek.

The ekphrastic poems were written in response to multimedia artworks, including painting, collage, short stories, photography, dance and music (what I'm defining as "auresis", or aural mimesis). Wherever possible, I've attempted to embody the formal elements of the work in addition to any descriptive component, and my thanks go to the following artists who were, either willfully or inadvertently, my collaborator on some of the poems. In all cases, I've included an epigraph from the artist in question to indicate their influence on my own generative process.

John Cage, Marc Chagall, Mel Chin, The Clash, Merce Cunningham, Edgar Degas, Rosemarie Fiore, Francisco De Goya Y Lucientes, Madsen Hartley, O. Henry, Edward Hopper, Phil Kline, Piet Mondrian, Joan Miró Mark Rothko, Ed Ruscha, Fritz Scholder, John Schott, Frank Sinatra, Sonya Sklaroff, Clyfford Still, Quintan Ana Wikswo, Francesca Woodman.

The italicized portions of *Maine Islands (1938)* come from Marsden Hartley's own poems; the parenthetical portions of *Course of Empire (2005)* are meant to evoke the jutting roofline of one of Ruscha's warehouses; the next note in John Cage's *As Slow as Possible* will be sounded on September 5, 2020 and after having lasted a duration of 639 years will finally end in 2640; Google Translate currently supports 90 languages, including Afrikaans, Chichewa, Esperento, Macedonian, Sesotho, Tamil and Yoruba; Phil Klikne's *Unsilent Night* is 45 minutes long, the length of one side of a cassette tape; Broca's area is a region in the frontal lobe of the brain linked to the production of speech; Rosemarie Fiore's firework drawings, like the one on this book's cover, were made by exploding live pyrotechnics in controlled bursts of saturated color; and I sat for Michael J. Peery's portrait of myself for nearly eight months and if the painting were to be x-rayed, you'd find other versions of me.

COLLABORATOR BIOGRAPHIES

Louis Bourgeois is the Executive Director of Vox Press, a 501(c)(3) arts organization based in Oxford, Mississippi.

Priya Sarukkai Chabria is a poet, writer, and translator who has collaborated with artists from Indian cinema, dance, and painting. See www.priyawriting.com; http://poetry.sangamhouse.org/about/.

Marc Chagall (1887–1985) was a Belarussian-Russian-French artist and an early modernist, referred to by art critic Robert Hughes as "the quintessential Jewish artist of the 20th century," who worked in several artistic mediums, including painting, book illustrations, stained glass, stage sets, ceramic, tapestries, and fine prints.

John Cage (1912–1992) was an American composer, music theorist, writer, and artist who pioneered indeterminacy in music, as well as electroacoustic and nonstandard use of musical instruments.

Mel Chin is a conceptual visual artist motivated largely by political, cultural, and social circumstances to calculate meaning in modern life.

The Clash was an English punk rock band that formed in 1976 as part of the original wave of British punk, and whose music incorporated elements of reggae, dub, funk, and rockabilly.

Merce Cunningham (1919–2009) was a dancer and choreographer known for his long-time collaboration with avant-garde composer John Cage.

Jim Daniels' latest books are *Birth Marks* (BOA, 2013) and *Eight Mile High* (Michigan State University Press, 2014).

Edgar Degas (1834–1917) was a French artist famous for his paintings, sculptures, prints, and drawings, especially identified with the subject of dance. He is considered one of the founders of Impressionism.

Daniel Donaghy is the author of two poetry collections: *Start with the Trouble* (University of Arkansas Press, 2009), which won the 2010 Paterson Award for Literary Excellence and was named a Finalist for the Milton Kessler Poetry Award and the Connecticut Book Award, and *Streetfighting* (BkMk Press, 2005), which was a Finalist for the 2006 Paterson Poetry Prize.

Sean Thomas Dougherty is the author of *Nightshift Belonging to Lorca*, a finalist for the Paterson Poetry Prize; *Except by Falling,* winner of the 2000 Pinyon Press Poetry Prize from Mesa State College; and BOA titles *Broken Hallelujahs, Sasha Sings the Laundry on the Line,* and *All You Ask For is Longing.*

Camille Dungy is the author of *Smith Blue, Suck on the Marrow,* and *What to Eat, What to Drink, What to Leave for Poison,* as well as the editor of the *From the Fishhouse* anthology and *Black Nature.*

Vernon Frazer teaches poetry and fiction and creates multimedia works that synthesize poetry and music with animated text.

Google Translate is a free, multilingual statistical machine-translation service provided by Google Inc. to translate written text from one language into another.

Francisco José de Goya y Lucientes (1746–1828) was a Spanish romantic painter and printmaker who worked as a painter in the Spanish royal court. He is well known for depicting the atrocities of the Spanish civil war.

Rosemarie Fiore is a pyrotechnic artist working in the Bronx who uses color smoke fireworks to produce large abstract works on paper.

Madsen Hartley (1887–1943) was an American Modernist painter, poet, and essayist whose work synthesized Cubism and other European modernisms with elegiac symbolism.

O. Henry (1862–1910), born William Sydney Porter, was an American short story writer known for his wit, wordplay, warm characterization, and clever twist endings. The title of the poem "A Square of Blue Infinity" is taken from a phrase in his "The Skylight Room" and the quoted section is taken from his "The Furnished Room."

Tiffany Higgins is the author of *And Aeneas Stares into Her Helmet* (Carolina Wren Press, 2009), with poems in *Poetry, The Kenyon Review, Taos Journal of Poetry and Art,* and *From the Fishhouse.* She writes on culturecology and has translated the work of several contemporary Brazilian poets.

Edward Hopper (1882–1967) was an American realist painter and printmaker who rendered memorable depictions of rural and urban life.

Frida Kahlo (1907–1954) was a Mexican artist who was married to Diego Rivera. She is known for the diaristic qualities of her self-portraiture.

Rodger Kamenetz is an award-winning poet, teacher, and author of eleven books, including *The Jew in the Lotus, To Die Next to You,* and *The Lowercase Jew.*

Lena Kallergi is a poet and translator who lives and works in Athens, Greece.

Phil Kline is an American composer who formed the New York No Wave band The Del-Byzanteens in the early 1980s, collaborated with Nan Goldin. His works often are moving sound sculptures.

Nancy Kuhl's third book of poems, *Pine to Sound,* will be published in 2014 by Shearsman Books. See http://www.phylumpress.com/nancykuhl.htm.

Frances Kai-Hwa Wang is a Chinese-American writer, educator, and activist who writes for ethnic new media and teaches writing and Asian Pacific American Studies. See franceskaihwawang.com.

Mong-Lan, Vietnamese-born American artist, poet, writer, painter, photographer, singer, dancer of Argentine tango, teacher, and winner of the Juniper Prize and the Pushcart Prize, is the widely anthologized author of eight books and chapbooks (www.monglan.com), including *Love Poem to Tofu & Other Poems* and *Song of the Cicadas.*

Megan Levad is the author of *Why We Live In the Dark Ages,* the inaugural collection in Tavern Books' Wrolstad Contemporary Poetry Series.

Harriet Levin is the author of *Girl in Cap and Gown* (Mammoth Books) and *The Christmas Show,* winner of the Barnard New Women Poets Prize and the Poetry Society of America's Alice Fay di Castagnola Award.

Reb Livingston is the author of *Bombyonder* (Bitter Cherry Books) and *God Damsel* (No Tell Books).

Piet Mondrian (1872–1944) was a Dutch painter, theorist, and draughtsman who evolved a nonrepresentational form that he termed neoplasticism.

Joan Miró (1893–1983) was a Catalan Spanish painter, sculptor, and ceramicist born in Barcelona. He is often considered a Surrealist for his recreations of the childlike and subconscious aspects of the human mind.

Eileen Myles is the author of eighteen books, including *Snowflake/different streets* (poems, 2012) and *The Importance of Being Iceland/travel essays in art*, for which she received a Warhol/Creative Capital grant. In 2010 the Poetry Society of America awarded Eileen the Shelley Prize and she's a 2012 Guggenheim fellow.

Alvin Pang is based in Singapore but has appeared at events around the world, been translated into over fifteen languages, is a fellow of the 2002 Iowa International Writing Program, and is the author of two volumes of poetry, *Testing the Silence* (Ethos Books, 1997) and *City of Rain* (2003) as well as the co-editor of several acclaimed anthologies, including the urban collection *No Other City: The Ethos Anthology of Urban Poetry* (2000) and the bilateral initiatives *Love Gathers All* (Philippines), *Over There* (with Australia) and *Doubleskin* (with Italy).

Clare Rossini is the author of three collections of poetry: *Lingo* (The University of Akron Press, 2006); *Winter Morning with Crow* (University of Akron Press 1997), chosen by Donald Justice for the Akron Poetry Prize and one of two finalists for PEN's first Joyce Osterweil Award; and *Selections from the Claudia Poems* (Minnesota Center for the Book Arts, 1996), an art book edition.

Mark Rothko (1903–1970) was an American painter of Russian Jewish descent who was one of the foremost members of the Abstract Expressionist movement. His work evokes strong emotions through abstract fields of color.

Ed Ruscha is an American artist associated with the pop art movement. He has worked in the media of painting, printmaking, drawing, photography, and film, recording the shifting emblems of American life in the last half century.

Fritz Scholder (1937–2005) is an enrolled member of the Luiseno tribe who sought to deconstruct the mythos of the American Indian. His revolutionary paintings forever changed the concept of the "Indian artist."

John Schott is a photographer, filmmaker, and academic whose 8x10 photographs of Route 66 from the mid-1970s were included in the exhibition *New Topographies: Photographs of a Man-Altered Landscape* at George Eastman House in 1975.

Frank Sinatra (1915–1998) was a Grammy award–winning American singer, actor, director, film producer, and composer.

Sonya Sklaroff is a contemporary American painter best known for her cityscapes of New York City.

Lisa Russ Spaar's most recent book of poems is *Vanitas, Rough* (Persea Books) and whose awards include a Guggenheim Fellowship, the Weinstein Award for Poetry, the Library of Virginia Award, and a Rona Jaffe Award for Emerging Women Writers.

Joseph Stanton's books are *Imaginary Museum: Poems on Art, A Field Guide to the Wildlife of Suburban O'ahu, Cardinal Points,* and *What the Kite Thinks: A Linked Poem* (a collaboration with Makoto Ōoka, Wing Tek Lum, and Jean Toyama.

Melissa Stein's poetry collection *Rough Honey* won the 2010 APR/Honickman First Book Prize, selected by Mark Doty, and was published by American Poetry Review in association with Copper Canyon Press.

Clyfford Still (1904–1980) was an American painter and one of the leading figures of Abstract Expressionism. His paintings use large-scale fields of color to evoke dramatic conflicts between man and nature taking place on a monumental scale.

Mónica de la Torre's latest publication is *The Happy End,* out from The Song Cave in 2014; she is senior editor for BOMB magazine.

Brian Turner is a poet and memoirist, whose latest book, *My Life as a Foreign Country*, is published by W. W. Norton and Company.

Quintan Ana Wikswo is an artist and writer whose projects span literature, photography, video, performance, interdisciplinary collaboration, critical theory, and activism. See www.QuintanWikswo.com.

Terri Witek is the author of *Exit Island* (2012); *The Shipwreck Dress* (2008), a Florida Book Award winner; *The Carnal World* (2006); *Fools and Crows* (2003); *Courting Couples,* winner of the 2000 Center for Book Arts Contest; and *Robert Lowell and LIFE STUDIES: Revising the Self* (1993).

Francesca Woodman (1958–1981) was an American photographer known for her self-portraiture and explorations of the human body, and whose untimely death only underscored the groundbreaking quality of her work.

The text of the book is typeset in 10-point Minion.
The book was designed by Lesley Landis Designs
and printed by BookMobile.